I08815495

★★★★★
MLB TEAMS

Texas RANGERS

KENNY ABDO

Fly!
An Imprint of Abdo Zoom
abdobooks.com

abdobooks.com

Published by Abdo Zoom, a division of ABDO, P.O. Box 398166, Minneapolis, Minnesota 55439.

Printed in the United States of America, North Mankato, Minnesota.
102025
012026

Photo Credits: Bridgeman Images, Getty Images, Shutterstock
Production Contributors: Kenny Abdo, Jennie Forsberg, Grace Hansen
Design Contributors: Candice Keimig, Neil Klinepier

Library of Congress Control Number: 2025936814

Publisher's Cataloging-in-Publication Data

Names: Abdo, Kenny, author.
Title: Texas Rangers / by Kenny Abdo
Description: Minneapolis, Minnesota : Abdo Zoom, 2026 | Series: MLB teams | Includes online resources and index.
Identifiers: ISBN 9798384940357 (lib. bdg.) | ISBN 9798384941118 (ebook) | ISBN 9798384941491 (read-to-me ebook)
Subjects: LCSH: Texas Rangers (Baseball team)--Juvenile literature. | Baseball teams--Juvenile literature. | Professional sports--Juvenile literature. | Sports franchises--Juvenile literature. | Major League Baseball (Organization)--Juvenile literature.
Classification: DDC 796.357--dc23

Table of CONTENTS

RANGERS

Blazing through the Lone Star State with grit and fire, the Texas Rangers leave rivals rattled and crowds roaring.

With big swings and bold plays, the Rangers round up wins and keep Texas fans riding high!

BATTER UP!

The Texas Rangers began play in 1961 in Washington, DC, as the Senators.

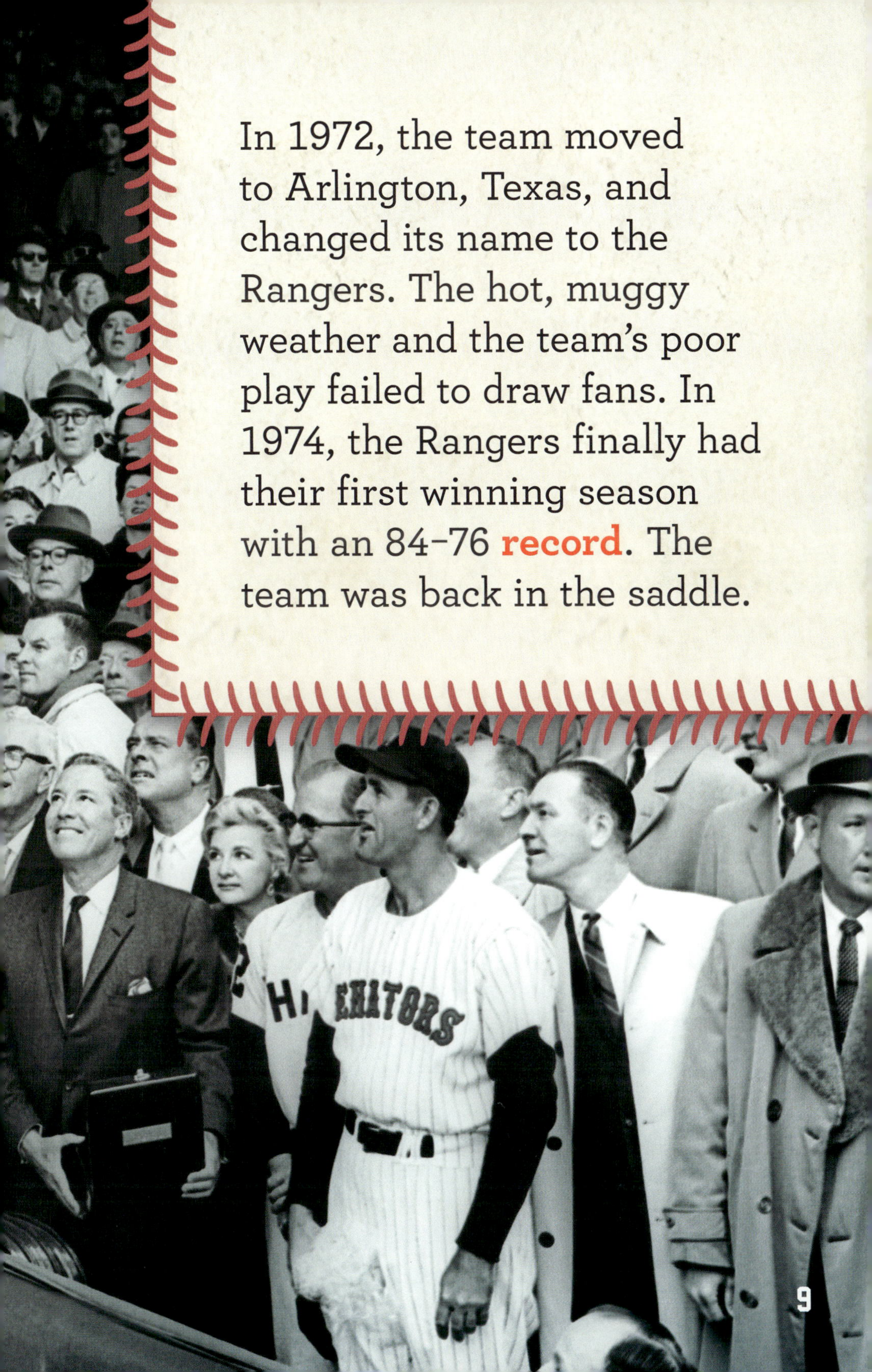

In 1972, the team moved to Arlington, Texas, and changed its name to the Rangers. The hot, muggy weather and the team's poor play failed to draw fans. In 1974, the Rangers finally had their first winning season with an 84–76 **record**. The team was back in the saddle.

T
TEXAS

The Rangers finally won their first **division** title in 1996. Iván "Pudge" Rodriguez hit .300 and scored 116 runs that season. But right fielder Juan González was the team's main power threat, hitting .314 with 47 homers and 144 **RBIs**. The Rangers made the playoffs again in 1998 and 1999.

By 2010, the Rangers were winners again. Josh Hamilton, a powerful slugger, helped lead the charge. The team defeated the Yankees in the **American League** (**AL**) Championship Series to move onto the World Series! They would lose to the Giants, but more thrills were just around the corner.

HAMILTON
32

GRAND SLAMS

The 2011 season was the best in team history. The Rangers won 96 games and made it back to the World Series to play St. Louis. The Rangers were just one strike away from a championship twice in Game 6 only to lose. Hamilton and Michael Young started Game 7 strong, but it wouldn't be enough. The Rangers lost 6–2.

From 2012 to 2016, the Rangers stayed strong. They won the **AL** West in 2015 and 2016. Prince Fielder and Rougned Odor delivered big hits, and Cole Hamels led the pitching staff. The team stayed a playoff **contender**.

The 2023 season was historic for the Rangers and its fans. The team surprised everyone by winning their first World Series title, defeating the Diamondbacks in five games. Shortstop Corey Seager won the World Series MVP. Seager had three home runs, three walks, six **RBIs**, and scored six runs in five games.

WORLD SERIES
MLB App
CHAPMAN
45
GROSSMAN
4
HEDGES
11
GARVER
18

Rangers

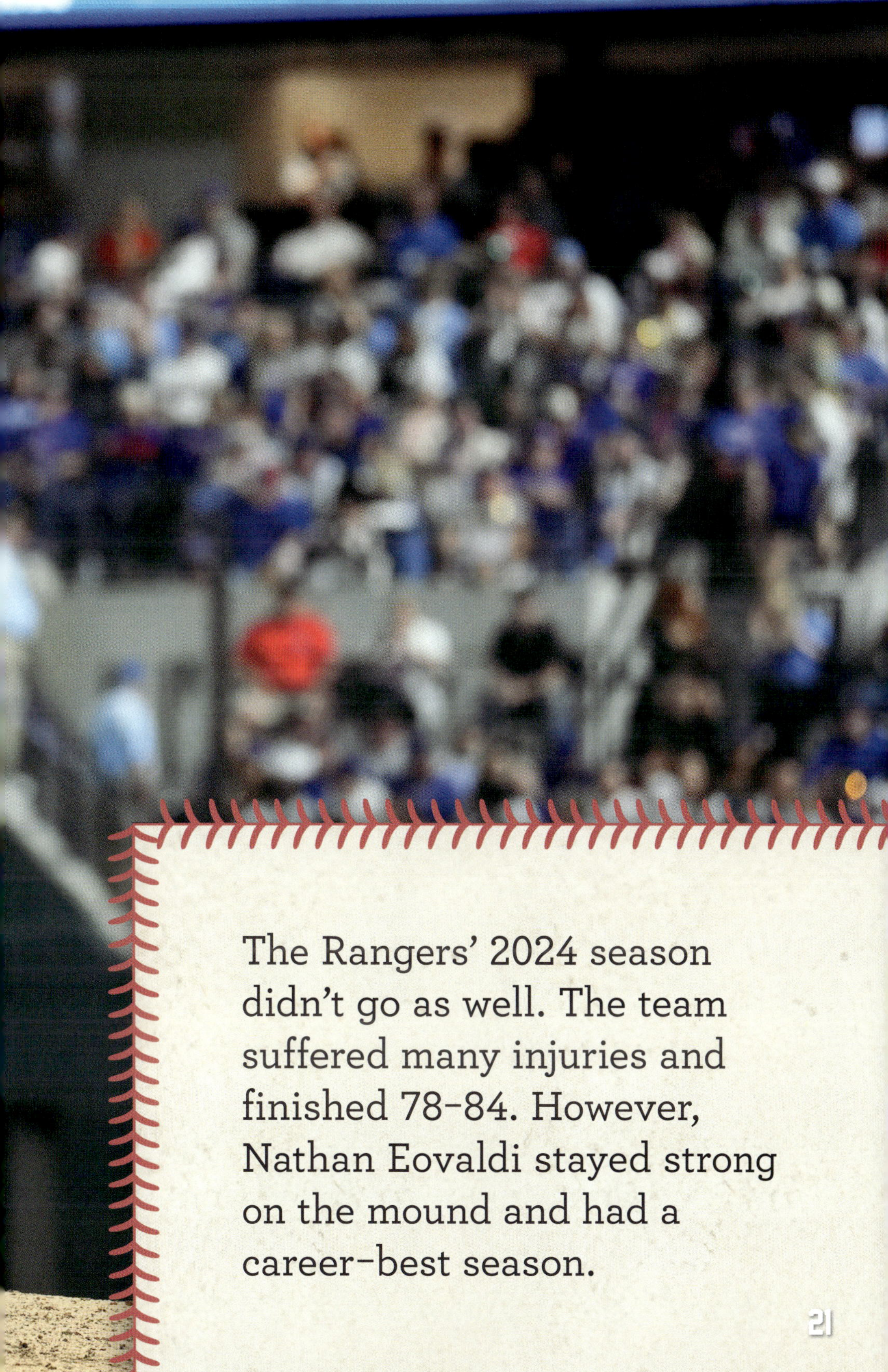

The Rangers' 2024 season didn't go as well. The team suffered many injuries and finished 78–84. However, Nathan Eovaldi stayed strong on the mound and had a career-best season.

GARCIA
53

In 2025, the Rangers celebrated **milestones** and defeat. Adolis Garcia hit his 140th home run as a Ranger. The team shined in pitching and defense. However, the offense lacked and the team finished with a frustrating 81-81 **record**. Still, fans hoped the team would soon find its way back to the top.

HALL OF FAME

Nolan Ryan was one of the greatest pitchers in baseball. He joined the Rangers in 1989. Ryan reached his 5,000th strikeout with the team. He was the first pitcher in Major League Baseball history to do so. Ryan helped bring national attention to the Rangers. He was named to the Baseball Hall of Fame in 1999.

PUDGE
Wilson

Iván "Pudge" Rodriguez was a star behind the plate and at bat. He won the 1999 MVP and helped the Rangers reach the playoffs for the first time in 1996. Known for his rocket arm and big hits, Pudge became a fan favorite. He finished his Rangers career with over 1,700 hits. Rodriguez was **inducted** into the Hall of Fame in 2017.

Adrian Beltré brought power, style, and a whole lot of fun to the Rangers. He smacked over 200 home runs with Texas and **dazzled** with his glove at third base. In 2017, he collected his 3,000th career hit. Beltré was loved for his big plays and bigger personality. He entered the Hall of Fame in 2024.

GLOSSARY

American League (AL) – one of two 15-team leagues that make up MLB.

contender – a competitor for a championship.

dazzled – to have amazed or impressed.

division – a number of teams grouped together in a sport for competitive purposes.

inducted – brought in as a member.

milestone – an important event or turning point for a team.

record – the total number of wins and losses a team has in a season.

Runs Batted In (RBI) – a statistic that credits a batter for making a play that allows a run to be scored.

ONLINE RESOURCES

To learn more about the Texas Rangers, please visit **abdobooklinks.com** or scan this QR code. These links are routinely monitored and updated to provide the most current information available.

INDEX